————————————

For The love

Of

The Art

————————————

Chyren Hayes

I

Cover Art by Gilbert Young

www.gilbertyoungart.com

all other images public domain

Keep it Moving Publishing

Atlanta, Georgia 2012

ISBN 978-0-9850319-0-9

www.chyren.net

Contents

Preface   **X**

Reality Poems Chapter   12

The Inspiration behind 2nd Half of Life   13

The 2nd Half of Life   **14**

The Inspiration behind All the Hell they catch   19

All The Hell They Catch   **20**

The Inspiration behind Sista Women Friends   22

Sista Woman Friends   **23**

The Inspiration behind Chyren Hayes   26

Chyren Hayes   **27**

Inspirational Poems Chapter   28

The Inspiration behind To Be Released   29

To Be Released   **30**

The Inspiration behind Through the Stress I smile   **32**

Through the stress I smile   **33**

The Inspiration behind The Lesson   **34**

The Lesson   **35**

The Inspiration behind Emancipated   **38**

Emancipated   **39**

The Inspiration behind Read the Signs   **41**

Read The Signs   **42**

Open Mic Nights Chapter   44

The Inspiration behind Feel Good Journey   **45**

Feel Good Journey   **46**

The Inspiration behind Travel the World   **49**
IV

Travel The World   **50**

The Inspiration behind Do you feel like that(part 2)   **54**

Do You Feel like that? (Part 2)   **55**

The Inspiration behind #2 Pencil   **59**

#2 Pencil   **60**

The Inspiration behind Two Loose Screws   **63**

Two Loose Screws   **64**

Notebook Poetry Chapter   68

The Inspiration behind Poetry For You   **69**

Poetry For You   **70**

The Inspiration behind If They Only Knew   **73**

If Only They Knew   **74**

The Inspiration behind I Wonder If it Pays   **75**

I Wonder if it pays   76

The Inspiration behind Church   78

Church   79

The Inspiration behind An Obvious Compromise   81

An Obvious Compromise   82

The Inspiration behind Hey Love   83

Hey Love   84

The Inspiration behind For The Love of The Art   85

For The Love of The Art   86

Love Poems Chapter   87

The Inspiration behind I Reminisce over you   88

I Reminisce over you   89

The Inspirations behind Brown Skin   93

Brown Skin   94

The Inspiration behind In this New Life of Mine   96

In This New Life of Mine   97

The Inspiration behind When I was in Love   99

When I was in Love   100

The Inspiration behind Right Here   102

Right Here   103

The Inspiration behind I love Her   105

I Love Her   106

The Inspiration behind From Far Away   109

From Far Away   110

The Inspiration behind I finally have found   111

I Finally Have Found   112

The Inspiration behind Young Sista   113

Young Sista   114

The Inspiration behind My Notebook and Me   116

My Notebook & Me   117

Lost Love Chapter   120

The Inspiration behind Suga Listen   121

Suga Listen   122

The Inspiration behind Matter of My Heart   124

Matters of My Heart   125

The Inspiration behind Don't Ask   127

Don't Ask Me   128

The Inspiration behind On This Valentine   130

On This Valentine   131

The Inspiration behind In Wonder Why   132

In Wonder Why   133

Acknowledgments   135

Story of Cover Art   136

Preface

For the Love of the Art is my first self-published book of poems. The impetus for this book was the brainchild of a 2003 website I created to lend exposure to my poems. The only stipulation I have is to show an inside look at the train of thought, inspiration and nuances that help to create a finished piece of work.

This book of poems is an introduction to Chyren Hayes and my unique style and perspective of writing poems. The selected poems are assembled by the date written, the story they tell, and the inspiration behind them, as well as my outlook and personal growth. My hopes are to invoke a feeling of familiarity that is relatable to the average person and provoke thought. Almost all of my poems are born out of an epiphany and a conviction of the story. Sometimes I introduce an idea or topic while in conversations to view others' perspective but all the while I am researching, reconciling or reaffirming my own views to identify a new truism.

The inspirations behind each poem will hopefully give some insight and make reading them just a little more interesting. For some people, the writings and the story they tell will stand by themselves while others will find new angles, meanings and maybe their curiosity will be satisfied by their knowledge of the poet's process in creating his work and drawing them into the poetic experience.

My poems by design are expressed in a simple direct fashion without a lot of tongue twisters and elaborate metaphors. I try to give my work a sense of spirituality that speaks parallel with clever words and builds to a final truism, beatitudes or philosophy. As I grow as a person in latitude, longitude, small and wide-angle frames, I would like for future publications and my entire catalogue to speak for itself and to some degree speak for me. I would like all criticisms and appreciations to be directed toward the work. My poetry can be best summarized by saying I am the teacher and the student at the same time. I am in awe and naïve to the ways and travels of man while offering my wisdom and cautionary vision.

ALL the HeLL THey Catch

Sista Women Friends

Reality Poems Chapter

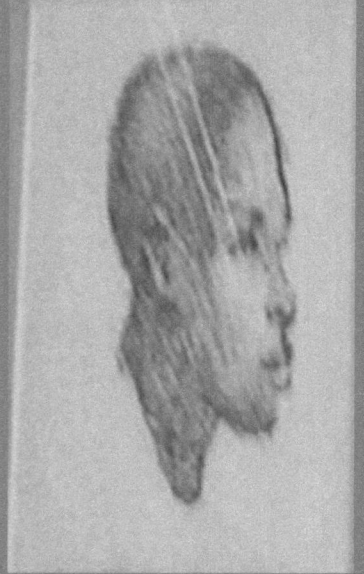

Chyren Hayes

2nd Half of life

The Inspiration behind 2nd Half of Life

The inspiration behind 2nd half of life is twofold. A friend I work with asked me to write her a poem talking about new outlooks, moving forward and having a new zest for life. She was in a space where she was ready to do all the things she had put on hold for so long. This poem was to be a catalyst or a manifesto of sorts to start her off and inspire her as she began this journey. The 2nd inspiration came from where I was in my life at that time. I had been having lots of financial difficulty that were really beating me up. And as I became more informed about economics, finances, classism and my American culture I began to have an opinion or philosophy. In order to have a well rounded view of a full life I knew that an elder my senior could give me some cautionary advise. I interviewed my Aunt Louise, my mother, my neighbor Mr. Bean, and 2 other elders. I took their wisdom as being true to their own life experiences and synthesized it into my own wisdom and understanding and came up with - The 2nd half of life. I really love what it is telling me and I aspire to live by its ideals. Oh and my co-worker Tracie says she likes it too.

The 2nd Half of Life

Good Afternoon hello and how are you?

Nice day that were having ahhhh! Look, the sun is shining,

Its clear skies and blue.

I hope looking back on your life the best of it is pleasant

And you got something out of it,

While you at least enjoyed yourself along the way.

I got some well needed refreshments, a few beverages

But more importantly lessons I can share with you any day.

I know early experiences, pot holes and detours got your love boat

dock at the shore. But in life, that's what their there for.

See you're doing something I already did

Let me tell you about where you're going.

It's called the 2nd half of life.

And actually it's so nice, a privilege, an honor

and an opportunity when you get to live it twice

Where the irony of it all is wild.

It parallels the never ever X-files.

If you live long encugh

you gon see it twice in a while.

From abstract to throwback,

the new sensation phenom to those old cats

Countless political improprieties,

religious transgressions and social societies.

From professional, intelligent, down to earth, dumb blind or crazy,

able bodied, crippled, all skin colors & 8 to 80,

benefactors and dream wishers,

from trading stocks to washing dishes

After a while you sorta learn to be keen to it.

To get to where I'm at and where you're going you're gonna need it.

You gotta kind of have an eye to; a mind to,

knowing when and when not to; when to push and when to hold still.

There's a whole 'nother definition to the word chill.

You couldn't know about responsibility until you first learn about will.

You couldn't know about hard work unless you know about bills.

You wouldn't know about having unless you haven't.

You thought pot holes was bad,

when you get older life keeps jabbing.

You might find yourself in traffic. Don't worry though,

Life gives you many tools & choices

you can use as an advantage.

But be careful you only get so many chances at it.

The main rule is to minimize the damage.

And the old adage is quite classic; Get'em while their young.

Nowadays you gotta start early getting your mind right.

You gotta start early getting your money tight.

You gotta give yourself opportunities and options

if you wanna last till the end of the 2nd half of life.

So as early as your teens years

you need to grasp the idea of economics or at least take a class.

Know the difference between race and social class.

Strap up, buckle down and put your back into it

during your working years, and I mean really.

Cause at twice, three times your age

it's gonna pay off and I mean really.

See there's no mystery to living leisurely, luxury comes at a cost.

When you get to the 2nd half of life

you might wanna be able to take some extended time off.

Whether your sick or you wanna take a trip,

You don't need no lip, no eviction slips

No wondering how you're going keep warm when Jack Frost hits.

Whether you got no health care or Medicaid,

the attention you get depends on how well your insurance pays.

And insomuch as you probably think I'm talking all that jazz,

There are no tricks involved.

There are simply normal and understandable outgrowths & conditions

that come with any windfall.

When you're up against your image

one day you'll see you never exercised lines and limits.

But you might really decide it's about time I read to achieve.

It's time I become a better me.

It's time I change up my wardrobe and set some new goals.

Patch up these old holes,

give back the time and the money I stole and wasted.

It's no wonder why I ain got shit.

I can't believe I didn't see it when I was younger.

But don't feel bad

it's only important that you actually someday

decided against complacency, ripping and running.

And then you'll really see

It's a Nice day we're having…

Ahhh look, its clears skies and blue..

Sit done and have some refreshments with me and let's talk about….

The 2nd half of life.

By Chyren Hayes © 1/3/08

The Inspiration behind All the Hell they catch

The inspiration beh nd All the Hell they catch is about a friend name Serena and my cousin Lamont. They used to be notorious for being mixed up in so many small time problems and just catching hell in what seems like everything they did. I was amazed by an idea of why some people do and some people don't. I don't think anyone catches that much hell without themselves having done something or not done something tc warrant it. I wrote this poem to tell myself that the things you do come back to you; Good and Bad. I hope they read this.

All The Hell They Catch

Have you ever looked at someone and see all the hell they catch

That motherfucker couldn't keep a job

If he owned the company and wrote the checks.

Why in the hell are they always down on their luck?

What seed did they plant that grows nothing but funk?

Taking from Peter to give to Paul, All the damn Time?

 Ain't that some shit?

All the Hell you catch and you haven't learned your lesson yet?

When you hear them they have stories like;:

I don't know where this bill came from,

I thought I paid those people

Oh My God! I can't even find my paperwork,

and they told me not to come if I don't have it.

The car was working fine yesterday

but this morning ch-gunk, ch-gunk.

They wrote me up because I was only two minutes late for work.

I wrote the check for the rent, but can you cash it next week?

I lost my D.L. Oh, I hope I left it at the bank.

I was just running the water in the sink, all of a sudden,

cl-clank, cl-clank.

I met this guy at the club who said they were hiring at his job

No, he wasn't trying to get with me.

I'm sorry, but can I reschedule my interview?

I locked my keys in the car and I can't make it today.

Oh shit, they got a road block,

and I was just going to pay my insurance next week.

Stories like these are all too familiar to some

If so, wake up, check yourself and what path you're on

Reading the signs is your best bet

It's something you're not getting from All the Hell you Catch

By Chyren Hayes © 2/2/00

The Inspiration behind Sista Women Friends

The inspiration behind Sista Women Friends was a friend of my mother's named Bootsie. One year I was visiting my family back home in Charleston. My mother always brags and talks about her kids to any person she meets. This day she was telling Bootsie that I wrote poetry. So of course she wanted to hear one. I recited a poem for their listening pleasure while they stood motionless listening.   And because of that impromptu display of messages in the words, I was commissioned to orchestrate a poem on Bootsies' behalf. I thought long and hard and couldn't find anything to write about because I didn't actually know this lady. I just met her that day. It took me about 3 months to find something that I felt would work. God blessed another one. Rest in peace Bootsie ('03).

Sista Woman Friends

I wrote this thinking about friends, Good Friends, Women Friends,

Not like Lucy and Linda or Katy and Kathy But Sistas,

Sistas like Cheryl and Cherisse or back home

I know Bootsie and Barbara.

These are Sista Women Friends

Who chit chat, who tell you like it is,

Who know all your biz, who know where you live,

Who know if your lying about who you say you is.

Who know if that's really your kid,

Who can tell you if you got it in you

Or if you need to add some more things to the menu.

Women friends who know what happened last night

Even though it was only one man and somebody else's wife.

Women friends who see in the dark like it was daylight

Who sit on the porch all afternoon

critiquing the neighborhoods' wrongs and rights.

But these Women Friends are people

who share something in common,

Something to talk about, something to laugh about,

Something to be concern over,

Something to be interested in and interested about.

They're people who share dreams,

Who share places. places they've been,

Places they wish they've been and places they've never been.

And things, things they've accomplished, things they've seen,

Things they've heard, things they've done

and things they wished they'd done.

These Sista Women Friends

share their last lifetime, summarize this one

And look forward to the next time.

 In one line they can tell you about your life and mine.

People who critique your shine,

who have words for the young mind,

the unsigned, the loose leaf, the slew-footed, the fly-by-night and especially those committed.

They share stories of love, first loves, second loves,

lost loves, firstborns and love scorn.

Sista Women friends give as much as they take

so it's easily accepted to each other how they love and hate.

Bootsie and Barbara are Sista Women friends

Life stories and experiences brings out the compassion within them

Nobody knows how long it will last

But when Sistas stop to talk, you know they'll be back

By Chyren Hayes © 6/19/01

The Inspiration behind Chyren Hayes

The inspiration behind Chyren Hayes is somewhat self involved. I wrote a few poems by this time and my friends were all giving me props. I had long wanted to do a poem boasting and bragging about who I was because my brother introduced me to Cash Money Millionaires and I always thought I could do that type of bragging in a poem to show him I got skills too. I also wanted to give it an eerie feeling that if something happened to me how would I be remembered in my own words. The poem "In the Event of My Demise" and various works by Tupac Shakur were a big influence. Looking at my collections of poems to date, I didn't have anything about me the person. I had poems about persons, places and ideas but none about the man himself. I put pen to paper and this is what came out. I want to be remembered for something more than just my SSN.

Chyren Hayes

I got more heart than a marine; a navy killing machine

An army size attack on a country to intervene

Far from in between and somewhere in forever

A story once told of a man who lived clever

Luxury was his pleasure and he treasured the greatest

Forever on a mission – At the top of his play list

Dealing with angles too acute to imagine

But discovering Blessings as he's living in Passion

Indubitably inclined to oblige in the laughter

Heaven and all its Glories is all he's really after

Written By Time – His Story is One of Enlighten

It seeps its way through the crevices of his writing

Stories of pain transcend into Constant Elevation Gain

The Enlightenment of His life shows in the Love he's obtained

By Chyren Hayes © 12/13/98

Inspirational Poems Chapter

Read The Signs

The Lesson

To Be Released

Through the Stress I smile

Emancipated

To Be Released

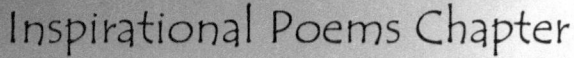

The Inspiration behind To Be Released

The inspiration behind To Be released is a close friend Serena. She was pregnant and had a miscarriage. We would talk often and only persons who has been through it can imagine how upset she was. She told me about the whole thing so I did what any friend would do; I tried to cheer her up. I came up with this poem to make her feel better and give some words of wisdom. As the poem says "postponed for a date undisclosed to the public" is a line to say she'll have another chance to have a child. Five years later Serena is now the mother of a beautiful little girl.

To Be Released

In your Days back to reality I know the realness of it hits

The overwhelming storm from whence calm decided to make a shift

But like in all black life there's a song for everything

I heard this un-released version that reminds me of your situation

It was a jazzy phat tune with a bass kick and drum snare

And the percussions in the background resonated through the air

The chorus had a hook that was perfect with the treble

And the girl who sung the song her name

was 'Elle' something something

It had crossover potential because of its conscious text

It's inspiration was motivating

because all of its words were sincerely felt

It was the type of song that could stand the test of time

And each time you heard it, it made you proud of who you were

Such an impacting inspiration sparked a social revelation

The community prompted the government

to change many of its legislation

Several entities of the administration

propagated the sor g's creation

And wanted to speak to someone important

preferably the song's originator

But the author to the song - Notably Serena Michele

Was a mere vessel for the inspiration - she was blessed as well

Final Production of the material was due out in October

Administration now sweating

knowing this is the New World Order

But the Most High saw it that the masses weren't totally fit

So the production is postponed for a date undisclosed to the public

So all is well that ends well

but now we're all waiting on the beginning

The vessel has been chosen

but the date To be released is still pending

By Chyren Hayes © 3/29/99

The Inspiration behind Through the Stress I smile

The inspiration behind through the stress is my faith. During
this period I believe I was feeling stress coming from my family,
relationships and my job. I can say for sure that during 1997 I became
extremely spiritual and became guided by it. God was strong in my life
and it showed in my writing. I also wrote Read the Signs and countless
other poems that reflect my strong spirituality during that time.

Through the stress I smile

As I journey this maze called mysteries of life

I'm frequently in contact with enemies of light

Bringing more stress more power than an "S"

It's a struggle not to buckle going through this stress

When everywhere I turn walls stand so tall

It's like I have no control and I always fall

But through all the madness of heartache pains

If I survive the storm I'll stand the rain

By Chyren Hayes ©3-17-97

The Inspiration behind The Lesson

The inspiration behind The Lesson is a self revelation. I wrote this poem for me about me. I became aware and grew tired that I was all over the place about women and relationships. I had been putting myself in awkward positions. Suddenly one day I got this clear meaning behind what was ailing me. I was being ailed because I didn't want to accept things I saw nor my own thoughts and feelings. I wrote this poem in probably two sittings. It tells all the insecurities I found in me and some I saw in others.

The Lesson

This right here has got to be The Lesson

Ever heard of a man that didn't know the answers to his questions

That didn't know the questions to his answers

That didn't know which question goes to which answer

Had an answer for every question

And each answer matched more than one question

Every question had to have an answer

And he knew exactly how to answer each question

And sometimes when he knew the answer to the question

There is something about him that he still has to ask the question

Some people come to him with questions

and expect him to answer them

Some people come to him with answers to their own questions

And some people come to him answers to his questions.

He's that kind of person that sits down and just finds questions.

Sometimes he'll pull a question out of the sky

He'll take that question, look at it

And put all of himself into answering that question.

He asks questions he knows he doesn't want to know the answer to

He asks the wrong people the wrong questions

Sometimes he listens to the wrong answers from the wrong people

If you ask him a question he'll answer it

But he doesn't really know the answer

Often times he ignores the right answers for the wrong reasons

And for the wrong reasons he'll just make up an answer

Sometimes he'll give you an answer and end it with a question!

If you ever meet a man

that doesn't know the answers to his questions

Tell'em this right here has got to be The Lesson

It's not all about so many questions

In fact questions really don't need answers

If you run into a question and you've got to get to guessing

Then the answer is not even worth stressing

Like Big Rube would say "Truth Be Told"

You already know the answer.

Tell'em he'll always be that same man

If he doesn't start off with a simple question

Look in the mirror and that will be The Lesson

By Chyren Hayes © 8/8/00

The Inspiration behind Emancipated

The inspiration behind Emancipated is a friend who I used to work with named Bob. He is a real cool guy. He told me about how he used to party so much back in the day and do all kinds of craziness young people would do. Anyone could see how he still has a semblance of playfulness and joy in him. But life can turn any of us into robots to some degree in order to maintain and take on the title of adults; and Bob is just another example. He married a long lost friend he said he once knew years ago and one day called her up and struck up a conversation and next thing you know they're married. That is a beautiful story if I ever heard one. About a year or so after I met Bob they were bringing a child into the world. As a gift I wrote and gave him this poem. I could see and feel Bobs' energy for love and life but more so his energy to be a better person for his child. I was extremely glad and proud that he loved the poem. He even framed it and put it up near little Bob.

Emancipated

Life is a journey through the sands of heavenly sacred time

Our exact whereabouts are unknown

in our minuscule space of mind

We are creatures that epitomize the true meaning of life itself

Glorifying good and bad in search of what we call self.

We are the triumphant as well as the conquered

Battles to the death some of us moving onward.

But as all journeys are somewhat alike-Life has a crossroad

Redefining complicity to simpality making clear ahead the road

For some it has past and others unexpectedly awaited.

The moment in life when all that ever was is Emancipated

I see your crossing and God Bless you in this half

He has brought you along thus far so there's no need to look back

They say confusion and chaos

will be people who you used to know

Becoming more familiar with peace

because she never came around before

Fear is now courage because Hope has been envisioned

Damn its amazing the biggest meanings now of the littlest things.

Guide this one with wisdom because now you have it to give

The journey through sand continues because now this life lives

By Chyren Hayes © 6/25/97

The Inspiration behind Read the Signs

The inspiration behind Read the Signs is my own belief about encouragement and faith. This poem came to me only as a title (as many of them do) mainly because I was thinking and stressing about on old relationship During that time I thought I was not going get her back because she was seriously involved with another guy. She always wanted to stay friends with me but that was hard for me and coerced so many different kinds of poems out of me. This poem is another example of that. I was always semi conscious enough to try not to be so obvious that my poems are directly related to or about me. But I want to try to transcend my own feelings and relationships into a lesson that someone else could use. I think you can too if you Read the Signs.

Read The Signs

I'd like to take this time to express my mind

About some things wide open and some hard to find

I get trapped in the between truth and disguise

Between Love Infatuation between Progress and Demise

I can't lie but I ain't always read the signs

I remember walking fast in the direction

to signs that read 'Deception'

You would think I would catch on

and make some kind of connection

But only fools pay the piper when they ain't never paid attention.

Sometimes my natural intuition had me more than just winning

Taking my destiny in my own hands is my primary mission

After I realized that God is the power and the glory

I've learned to read the signs

and watch my life play out like a story

It took me some time to know how to read the signs

But when you go wrong the first time

that's a clue from the most high

Like maybe when you least expect it

That thing you wanted starts connecting

That's the sign, clear as day, all you got to do is start stepping

Because when you take advantage of his Bless

You'll know the Lord for yourself

And when the times ain't easy, This is where you can rest

So I'm putting it on paper to make it known to my God

That I hear you talking and thank you for the cue cards

Now till forever

I pray to see what you ask and what you give to me

And pass it on to the next so they'll know to read the text

So thank you for letting me share this time,

I'll keep moving and keep reading the signs.

By Chyren Hayes ©1999

Feel Good Journey

Do You feel like that Sometimes

Travel The World

Open Mic Nights Chapter

#2 Pencil

Two Loose Screws

The Inspiration behind Feel Good Journey

The inspiration behind this poem came from hearing the instrumental of a song by Ge-ology[1] called Inebriated (feel good journey) from the album THE RADIO IS TEACHING MY GOLDFISH JU-JITSU. I play a lot of instrumentals when I'm in the lab just to escape my issues. This is also around the time I started to experiment with writing in 16 bar verses instead of just a long spoken word piece. I was looking for a way that I could challenge myself as writer. I had different verses lying around in different parts of my notebook. Individually the verses never really spoke to a point of view that I felt made any sense besides vanity so they just sat there. Until one Saturday morning I got up and played that instrumental and wrote the first verse to match the bars of the song. I tried the other verses I had and the rest is what you hear. I added the singer in later to give the song it's just due.

Feel Good Journey

It aint nothing but a thing to me how we do this over here

Me, myself and I are well aware

How the pen passion is sweet but the poison with catch your hear

The flow starts waving at you like

You might wanna come see bout this brother over here

Words and verbs flow like a dutch

Sentences and paragraphs feel good to touch

I'm like a painting by Frank Morrison[2] "The last call"

Or John Holyfied[3] – I'm a Poet ya'll

Transmitting this right where I stand

Thank full this morning God woke me up again

To let you know ,It feels good writing again

In the night time I write aesthetic rhymes

Pleasing to hear and soothing to the mind

[2]www.morrisongraphics.com
[3]www.holyfieldstudio.com

It usually starts off with a clever line

Then an improbable amounts of combinations

Is left up to the imagination of my mind

I flow like your watch got the time

Like a white cloud in a blue sky

In my notebook this is page 4079

Where the topics range like the day change

I'm contemplating one now about the shade

Right after this one I just finished about the babe

This poem is really about a prophet in rage or a poet-at-large

Either title I go by I got'em both printed on my card

Along with my sky miles and the # of notebooks I've put down

Going through my everyday just comes ideas

Catch phrases about persons, places and ideas

That brings me back to the night time and me

In the lab where its fully staffed

with hooks feel good lines and vibe

I'm just a poet walking With words that be talking

In sections where I give'em rhythm

Trying to give'em vivid pictures

Using my time to write prescriptive rhymes

Lines that are contrived from the times

At the same time trying to manage mine

Keeping a hold of my good line

Using my gray matter to say something that matters

Whatever time I got left I'm using the latter

Keeping your hands open means more coming inside

I know about the vices and the trials

The insecurities the obstacles and the long mile

The let down, the set backs and the reverting back

But no matter how many times you never should get used to that

And that's where I'm at in 2006

God bless another one and you can ride out to this

By Chyren Hayes ©2005

The Inspiration behind Travel the World

The inspiration behind Travel the World is a song called Respiration by a rap group named Blackstar[4] (Yassin Bey & Talib Kweli) with a guest spot from Common[5]. I was particularly inspired by a line from Common who said "I ask my guy how he thought traveling the world sound, found it hard to imagine he hadn't been past downtown". Anyone who is into to hip-hop knows this rapper and this group has many hip notables quotes. The whole song struck me when I first heard it. It was on regular rotation for a long time in my car. I took what that line meant to me and tried to transcend it into a poem about an old man giving advice to the listener. I imagined myself being an old wise man talking to a young brother. I dedicate this poem to my younger brother Marion (P-nut).

Travel The World

I was speaking to this old man and I asked him

How he managed to travel the world and stay sound

He looked to me and said "Chy like Tupac- I get around"

He said I know that feeling like it aint no get right on the get back

Like you gotta take a lost just to get some act right

Like an honest man claim to fame

is always his struggle to maintain

It seems like hard times is like the grand groove

And everybody I know is catching the beat

You gotta do so much to make the drama miss you and miss me

He said one day he just got tired of the same old same

The pressures of life, personal strife

So He left looking for a change

Saying there had to be something better than this

Better than this trip, this lick, this $2 trick

So he packed up all his shit and crossed over the tracks

To see how they do it uptown, downtown,

eastside and the westside

Wallstreet, Capital Ave and Technology way

New Jerus, and places where even Mexicans sing the blues

He said he shot pool with the mayor and ate fine food with killers

Was blessed by The Dioceses with 3 Hail Marys

Because all of us are born sinners.

He talked to me about "The Jones"

and why their grass always stayed green

Said Bitches and niggas are worldwide,

different from men and women

you just gotta identify'em

He said all white people don't aim for the neck

And those that do are simply scared of you

Keep you hands open because you can't get nothing in if its closed

And that's a figure of speech so share

and let some of that stuff you got go

He gave unto himself all the lessons he had learned

If you didn't know any better it sounded like clichés and warnings

Like a Sunday morning song on a Friday night

You either was waiting for end or using it for some inner light

He said I aint the man I used to be but I'm still the same man,

laughing with a smile, (Pause) Boy I'm just on a different plan

You wanna know how I travel the world and manage to stay sound

Well everybody got the same problems,

just in degrees is how it goes around

Take this one or that one the white one or the black one

Pick the person it's just a question of action

What you gonna do when stress comes to you

Either you gonna knuckle up or pass out, face off or ass out.

Pray on it for 3 days and then rise

You really gotta talk to your God in the sky.

So I replied with a head node and said true

 Alright Ok. Alright OK. Alright OK...I'm feeling you.

So now I just press on through the mush

and I don't throw my hands up as much.

It's because thanks to the old man

I'm trying to travel the world and not get stuck.

By Chyren Hayes ☺2002

The Inspiration behind Do you feel like that(part 2)

The inspiration behind part 2 of this poem is musical. Sometime around 2004 I got the idea to start using instrumental hip-hop to perform my poetry. This brings me to when I heard this song that was included as a sampler to some cd I bought online. When I first heard the song it struck me where I was standing and I just had to use it. I used a sampling software called ACID and tweaked it to extend the length. From there I searched through what poems I had as well as tried to write a new poem but after reading part 1 of this poem I knew it would work. I knew I needed to lengthen the poem to go with the song so I worked and worked on it as I rode the train to work every day and God blessed me with something I was pleased with. This is the first poem I used this technique with and others soon followed. The subject matter is about what I see with those who actually handle and juggle the responsibilities of life. Being an adult sometimes is no fun. I heard Abiodun from The Last Poets[6] say that. I hope you feel the words in this poem because I still do.

[6]http://en.wikipedia.org/wiki/The_Last_Poets

Do You Feel like that? (Part 2)

Often times in the forefront of my mind

I'm contemplating the world

And just looking at from a distance,

yet in still I walk amongst all its ills

I see half life and half trife, heavy burdens and weary nights

So much so I search for peace when I'm gazing at a starry night

Treading the urban concrete hurts because

I see the brick side of things

I see the joy & pain in their hurt when the choir is in full swing

I see the conviction in their eyes

when they hope for the best of things

I see how people relate to any song when any artist starts to sing

I see insecurities masked by so many different kinds of things

I see physiological, descent zed,

psycho-neurotic, psycho-psychotic

Its messed up because Truth be told I feel like I got it

I wonder at angles of acute degrees

Understanding more and more why older people plant trees

It gets to a point where I have to exhale and breath

So I just go back to the lab and kick back

Put on some electric relaxation

Chant a Psalm or get in some meditation

Play some instrumentals and I'm off ...to unknown destinations

Escaping the light scrapes and the deep bruises

Being under appreciated and overused

The juggling act of home, work and school

Bills, relationships and political news

The facade of the American dream unravels a tapestry of deceit

Seen on all levels local, federal, executive and especially discreet

All my peoples are doing their best to just hold on

It seems like that's our favorite song

With repercussions and vices and addictions

You're really only somebody until you buck the system

A midst of the stair steeping

Hill climbing, wal riding and mountain peaks

An increasing pressure builds as circumstances increase

Options diminish, avenues get shorter and resources run low

Necessity runs into morality collides and strickens the flow

Then spirits get weary and essences become weak

While burdens on shoulders fall to feet

Exhaustion and lack of sustenance cause muscles to contract

Low pressure with no salt and now images dim black

And paramount to any high drama you see on TV

It's all channel live in 3D, the urban concrete, you, me and us three

No script to follow fashion, no director or action cam

Everybody I know dealing with superhero type problems

And we're just a regular man

With two shoulders and two hands but carrying buildings

And I hate to be speaking in a starving artist tone

But like bob Marley all I ever have are redemption songs

I'm looking for any light to write a brighter poem

Holding on to after thoughts of faith to write a living psalm

They say it's all an earned conversion the trouble and the hurting

If you don't go through it

you won't know meaning of what's worth it

You may find it enlightening but maybe that's just my state of mind

I wonder though, Do you feel like that sometimes?

Chyren Hayes © 08/17/05

The Inspiration behind #2 Pencil

The inspiration behind # 2 pencil is an extensive and challenging period of time where I was trying to find out exactly what it is I can and can't do and the difference between poetry and spoken word. Sounds like a lot of unnecessary worrying for a brother that pays his five dollars to get on stage for 4-5mins and walks off without anyone being able to pronounce, remember or even say my name or my poem (oh yes it happens). I don't know if it's the talent pool here in Atlanta that keeps a poet on his toes or my own picking and prodding. I wrote this poem with current events in mind, namely the incident with the straight guy that harassed a gay guy at Morehouse and my strong feelings on paying to perform at an open mic. I felt like poets at open mics weren't appreciated or at least I wasn't. I felt like poets on the scene all had the same style and were talking about things with no strong substance. I saw people applauding to things that seemed so simple. I sadly report to you I tried to fit in that style. This poem came out of that.

#2 Pencil

Under the clear skies of a crescent moon

The lunar moves me to reminisce and soon

I'm sitting back thinking, enjoying situations

Having a few laughs, conversatin' and yeah Occasionally dating

Living as I'm learning and you heard Andre 3000[7], They testin.

Got my #2 pencil and my God as The weapon

A fearsome sum that makes them all Succumb

But that's an introduction to another one

This mic stresses my ability to jest to, relieve stress

Sitting here at home just writing mess

Thinking about this, that and the third

My Ex-girl, my old bird and of course Spoken Word

That Morehouse junk got me upset and sad

I wasn't there but I'd say he was trying to get some ass

Now my man doing 20 and I'm not saying he's right

Because threaten somebody with a bat is some gangsta type

[7]www.outkast.com

But on forward let's talk about differences

6 degrees of separation and how big that really is

My Guess Art is Ertertainment if the audience pays a fee

The Club and the Bar split the profits

and satisfaction depend on me (we)

Open-Mic nights is nice but I work hard at night

Bleeding out these Ghetto poems

with courage to perform them under these lights

Its time to Organize Confusion and specialize in the Art the Pays

Getting paid for what you love is the name of the Game

So…Introducing …Chyren …sit back and let me tell you

I Capture a moment like a vibe with a spirit that moves you.

Smooth like a breeze unnoticed I go by

I really just wart to uplift people, places and ideas when I write.

So until the next clear sky under a crescent moon

I'll be enjoying situations

Having a few laughs, conversatin' and yeah occasionally dating

Living as I'm learning and you heard the man, They Testin

Got my Table of Contents, My God and my #2 pencil.

By Chyren Hayes ©6/13/03

The Inspiration behind Two Loose Screws

The inspiration behind Two loose Screws is sort of a personal revelation. Just like the next person I experience life for all its good, bad times and have my own insecurities. One issue I was dealing with was trying to tell the difference between not committing to a woman because I just wasn't feeling her on that level or not committing because physically she wasn't attractive enough or being attracted physically but mentally they don't do it for me. I thought back to some of the sistas I've dealt with and at the time I wrote this poem I was dealing with a sista that was massaging me mentally. I was feeling her and comparing her to what I wanted physically. Thinking about this whole thing one day I came up with the title Two Loose Screws. The title was just a catchy phrase to get the people's attention but it also paints the picture. This poem is one of those chosen few poems that highlight the pure reasons why I write and where I write from when the intentions are pure. Poems that come from that pure place have changed and encouraged my makeup as a person and I hope to create more poems to point out those little intricacies I think we all go through because at the end of the day we all have at least Two loose Screws.

Two Loose Screws

She was a Perfect 10 from a distance

And none less the least I expected

Perfection from this Immaculate Conception

Whisper talks of how fine she compliments a line

In a poem of mine, something lovely skin pure

Not a hair line fracture or bone spur

And best believe, Yes sir I'm mack'n her

So we're building conversation like we're raising children

Reading Cornel West "Prophetic Fragments"

and listening to Kelsy Davis[8] "Soup and Syrup"

But from all the blur clearly I started to see her

And boy you just ain' know she had me fooled from the door

See she couldn't divide a thousand by two

Ask her for change for a dollar, she give you back two

But hellified in matching her pants to her boots

[8]www.myspace.com/kelsydavisradicalsoul

But that's cool, I'll just keep moving but I got this theory proven

All good things don't last not even a full tank of gas

Its true take a closer look at your left shoe

It doesn't fit exactly like the right, not even a pair of gloves fit right

But more true is we all come with at least 2 loose screws.

Now there was this suite that fit me dead fresh to the Tee

Crafted and stitched with labor and sweat

Abstract – patterns no one had ever seen yet

And I'm out to be seen like a Blackstar imagine this

Shining like who on top of this

7 piece get-up with the a cuff and a crease

Yoke the joker wait till they get a load of me

My handkerchief match the tie and the belt match the shoe

My head clean and nails done so

"Dat boy sharp" basically is the tune.

But expectations always outlast performance

Because the loose string inside the suite pocket shows it

And that's cool, I'll just keep moving but I got this theory proven

All good things don't last not even a full tank of gas

Its true take a closer look at your left shoe

It doesn't fit exactly like the right, not even a pair of gloves fit right

But more true is everything comes with at least 2 loose screws

Now this one close to me like my love for writing verses

Integral to my development like writing in cursive

Now it hurts but they say that's just what the truth do

Someone near to me like a hug got a few screws loose

My young eyes would stare up at authority

Lovingly, homely providing guidance to me

Teaching me how to walk straight and fly right

Instructing my wisdom on hard days and long nights

But why the teacher lessons only good for the student

Telling me not to and you turn around and do it

Maybe it's the point of the matter and you have been here longer

It did keep me from unnecessary drama

I can see that now since I'm older

But I've come to realize and it's cool,

Imperfection is the only one truth

Just like parents do the Best they know how to do

Like All good things don't last not even a full tank of gas

Its true take a closer look at your left shoe

It doesn't fit exact y like the right, not even a pair of gloves fit right

But more true is everyone, everything and All,

comes with at least 2 loose screws.

By Chyren Hayes ©2/04/04

Poetry for u
If Only They Knew
For The Love of The Art
NOTEBOOK POETRY
I wonder if it pays
Church
On Obvious Compromise
Hey Love

The Inspiration behind Poetry For You

The inspiration behind this poem is another day of looking for inspiration and trying to find it. I wrote this poem sitting in a small little cafe' on Cascade road called Eclectic Cafe'. This cafe is real smooth because along with serving brunch and eclectic dinner entrees it has a lot of black art all over the walls and plays smooth sounds over the airways. That's one thing about living in Atlanta I love is there is always a spot that you can find that is on some other level. I was here because I was trying to relax my mind to find a poem I could use for a poetry show I was planning. At that time I was working heavy on putting together a group of poets I wanted to showcase under a theme. The theme was to be Poetry For You:7 Poets 7 styles. I came up with the idea that I'd open the show with a poem that would fit that theme. I wrote this all in one sitting. I guess you can say I was hyped because of working on a show. I don't think it is as full or as strong as I'd like it to be but no matter how many times I go over it there seems to a part of me that wants to leave it as is while the other part wants to strengthen it. I decided after a long struggle and a deep breath to just leave it is as and let the chips fall where they may because after all it is Poetry For You.

Poetry For You

It's For You

It's Poetry For You

For those who never knew what it is

What it could do

What it could change

What it makes you think

What reactions it cause

What understanding it evolves

What emotions it calls

It's All For You

It's Poetry For You

For Sistas, Brothas, Mothers, Fathers

Sons and Daughters, Young and Elders

This is for the tall dark and handsome

Or short brown ar d them some

For the trendy, cosmopolitan, old school, old soul

Gun-ho, loud & rude and quiet and smooth

This is for the slender & sleek and curvaceous curves

No ass-a-tall and booty bouncing off the wall

It's all

For You

It's Poetry For You

This is for your listening pleasure

Relaxation, enjoyment and satisfaction

This relieves stress and a getaway from the mess

Dis a whole other set abstract poetics

Social elements, a lovers best, revolutionary threats

Self-identifying checks, group awareness is always a bless

Pictures painted that stand the test

It's all more or less

For You

It's Poetry For You

This for the jaded and incarcerated

The railroaded and alienated

For the lost & unknown with no way back home

Back broken, spirit hurting heart yelling eyes swelling

The admonished and outcast the exiled

Most importantly

This is to make you laugh and smile

To wonder like a child

To exercise innocents and release

An unconscious reaction to exhale with peace

I pray at least

It's all

For You

It's Poetry For You

By CHYREN HAYES ©7/30/03

72

The Inspiration behind If They Only Knew

The inspiration behind If They only Knew was at the time I got tired of family and certain friends saying that they knew I was a certain type of person. Say I would react this way in this situation or that way in that situation. I felt like I'm the person I need to be when I need to be but its hard to convey that to someone who has their mind made up on what they think about you.

If Only They Knew

This one is dedicated to the One Shots and the Last Call

The Worldly Wise who think they've seen it and done it all

Those who say they call it like they see it

And if they don't believe it then you can't be it

The one tracks who swore they knew a true fact

But all the while underestimated what I might be, Imagine That.

Had me mapped out like a plan with no options like a sedan

If Only They Knew it's so much more to being An Honest man.

BY Chyren Hayes © 2/3/01

The Inspiration behind I Wonder If it Pays

The inspiration for this poem is based on my ever present duality between questioning religion and an intro/retrospective view of my own life. When I first wrote it I was scared of it because I felt like it was disrespectful to my own God. But I got to thinking and felt that well maybe god knows his kids sometimes ask questions. And for the sake of what I do which is to present feeling and ideas, I believe we all go through the same thing. So I put this poem out there. I have performed this piece on stage once and as I'm writing this I think I should do it again. I hope you like it.

I Wonder if it pays

You know they say keep your head up, be strong and hold on

You gotta keep it moving, read the signs and always stand strong

If you make it through the night who knows what'll be tomorrow

Just one hopeful prayer away,

To end all your terrible troubles and seeping sorrows

But I wonder if it pays? If it's all in vain or it really is Glory Days

I wonder if it depends how many times I went to church on Sunday

Or it really is true about giving 10% of your salary

I wonder if my mother did the crime means I gotta do the time

Why when out of the blue a life turns tragic

When just a second ago it was fine

I wonder if it pays?

Sunday school, early service, deacon board and youth choir

When crack just took a part of my family tree

Or coming home from church I found my house on fire

Why living from check to check and on some days I don't even eat

I even wonder if it pays to say grace before I sit down to eat.

Maybe it's odds on end with the best man to win

3 cents on a dollar or a 1000 to 1 if you really wanna holler

Maybe it pays every 7yrs on 7th month on the 7th day at 7 o'clock

Full moon rising, beware since I paid now I'm in for all the luck

I wonder if it pays 4 x's a year to every other person measure in degrees

Maybe 1 person per household every 90 days and void if overseas

I wonder if it matters that I thought it best to take the long route

Disregarded the so easy and volunteered my time to help another out

Maybe it depends on what you did Saturday night

Or what you do right after you walk outside of the church doors

If you get served right

Maybe II Timothy 2:21 is completely right and exact

God Forgive for any disrespect. I just wonder if it pays?

A question a young soul had to ask.

By Chyren Hayes © 10/23/01

The Inspiration behind Church

The Inspiration behind Church was satisfaction. I was in the church pew when I wrote this as the service was going on. I was feeling very happy to be in church because I hadn't been there in a while. I was reveling in the joy I was feeling and looking around to see how certain things are a staple in a church and won't ever change. When I was finished I was so happy that I nudged the person next to me and let her read it. She probably thought I was having the holy ghost of something. Or was I? Things that make you say hmmmmm. Ha ha ha.

Church

The Preacher is still Preaching

The Deacon is still Teaching

The Choir is still Singing

The Usher is still Greeting

The Music is still Playing

The Pastor is still Praying

People are still Coming

Kids are still Running

Babies are still Crying

Touched People are still Crying

Holy Matrimony in Gods Eyes

Heaven is still Just above the Skies

A Few Good words and a smile when they die

The Sermon still makes me wanna cry

I'm always a different person when I walk outside

Genesis to Revelation prophesied since way back when

God Blesses us all… and The people still say Amen.

By Chyren Hayes © 10/29/00

The Inspiration behind An Obvious Compromise

The inspiration behind this poem was boredom one day at work. I normally construct my poems with pen and paper but I tried typing on the computer since I didn't have anything better to do. The meaning came from thinking and wishing people will one day study my work and my life. And they would come up with all these analyses of me and find out insightful things through my work. Maybe that's wishful thinking but I do hope for that.

An Obvious Compromise

It's an obvious compromise

The affair between her and I

One loves to speak the other rarely says hi

One goes where it wants the other is satisfied on the side

One can uplift and transcend

the other is narrow even through magnifying lens

One mingles and draws attention

the other is withdrawn and not to mention

One is weak and insecure and

the other is bold strongly inspired by the earth

They exist within a union that organizes confusion

A dichotomy relationship that's mutual and exclusive

But the one epic single winner is undistinguished and elusive

So in the immortal words once spoken

The Saga Continues…

By Chyren Hayes ©7/22/04

The Inspiration behind Hey Love

The Inspiration behind Hey love is just a freestyle approach after listening to a song from A tribe called quest[9]. Even now I'm still learning to know when I'm just rambling words or when I'm on to something that could be a solid poem with substance. This poem struck me. I wrote almost all of the lines in one sitting. Each time I read it the feeling I get is one of honesty and truthfulness. I usually try to shoot for something that is at least one page long but truth be told sometimes I try to wrap up and close any unfinished poems so that I can start new ones. And trust me it's not as careless as it sounds

Hey Love

I'm an Artist and I write what I feel

I write what I like as If I'm free to be what I might

I feel like I might just be what I put into words last night

So strong it felt like I got enticed to write

It built up inside me pushing and I'm like aiiright, aiiright!

Inspired and with ideas, walking up spiritual stairs

If I wasn't where I was supposed to be

Then these words wouldn't have ears

Hey love let me tell you about my only vice

It has to do with lots of writing and it can be so nice.

By Chyren Hayes © 4/7/01

The Inspiration behind For The Love of The Art

The Inspiration behind For the love of the Art came at a jazz club in Atlanta called Churchill Grounds[10]. On Tuesdays they have Jam Sessions and open the stage and the instruments to other jazz musicians, vocalist and sometimes poets to jam with the house band as they go throuch various standards. To this point in my experiences I had only been to spoken word open-mics. At Churchill grounds I saw black and white ranging in ages from young to elder. I was taken aback by watching older musicians come to the stage w/their instruments. I said to myself this reminds me of what I see poets do. Poets go to varicus places to get on the mic to get that release and satisfaction. I found that all of us(poets and musicians) being talented to various degrees and the hustle is the same. We get off work and come out to these venues to do something that's not paying us and for many all we have is our day job. The feeling caught me to see the love that all artists have for their art. We only really do it for the love for the art.

For The Love of The Art

And I know its for the love of the Art

The late nights with no recognition has gotta be hard

At lest they know my name at my day job

A small room with a dim light

is all that's left of being young unsigned and hype

and now I'm just hype

and my only buzz is Corona w/lime.

And my only promotion is

the MC saying "Introduction to the stage one time"

And now I'm...really only it for the love of the art

The late nights with no recognition yeah its hard

But the words and sounds free my soul now

And my day job is actually the thing that's odd and hard

The love of the art,

Yeah we really only do it for the love of the Art.

By Chyren Hayes ©11/15/05

When I was in Love

Right Here

My Notebook & Me

New
Life of Mine

Love

I love Her

I reminisce over you

From Far Away

Young Sista

I finally have found

Brownskin

The Inspiration behind I Reminisce over you

The inspiration behind this poem had to do with frustration. I had been trying very hard to write a poem that was coherent and fluid but I kept coming up short with lots of half verses or lines that didn't combine to say anything worthwhile. This still happens every now and again. I decided on this day that I'll just write about something that I have lots of feelings on. This may sound like a natural thing but I made a promise to myself sometime ago to not keep harping on my past and what not. This time I made an exception just to get my MUSE back and this is what came out. This poem is (was) currently being performed over an instrumental smoothed out hip-hop track by Black Skramm[11]- The archive scavenger. Trust me it's maad smooth.

I Reminisce over you

I'm reminiscing over a time

Where I can't forget to remember because it was so cool

A day etched by a memory

Of a sequence of events that altered my stroll

This la-di-da brown koffee cinnamon sugar was nutritious

With hips curves and thighs

Had a flavor oddly different yet delicious

I'm a man blessed with insight

Looking at her clearly I see right

Into her bright wide mahogany eyes

Queen Amina aint had nothing on my Rena

But it wasn't just about physical looks

But demeanor and attitude

Speaking about life and love and telling me I can pull though

And from where I'm from

they don't talk like that when there that young

So the honesty in wisdom is telling me that this maybe the one.

Chorus:

repeating the same to myself last night

As I think back to a time where I can't forget to remember

Because it was so cool.

I wonder who, now and how she getting though

Cause fa real I reminisce over you.

Courtship was like a poem I never wrote

You can't script a natural thing

It gotta do what it do baby

Like Ray Charles would say

So we did all kinds of things

Traveling without a car, bus or plane

Good Conversations is a trip aint it?

Like the soft drops of the falling rain

We had hard times, happy, awkward, new

Bad and sad but God said true

And just as the lord giveth he taketh away

Leaving behind a soberness of reality

Today don't seem nothing like yesterday

And the tear drops on my window pain

Say so much more than a poem can ever say

And it's so strange what life and circumstances take us through

Chorus:

And I wonder why

So I write a few lines I can feel but all that comes out is

how I reminisce of you fa real.

As Time brought change,

A few things have while other stayed the same

I'm still doing tricks on my bmx kicks

Using crayons to paint pictures with words that fit

Still describing moods and carving my niche

in this open mic groove

Still super cool like a senior on the 1st day of school

Using my religion to make the rough edges smooth

Still a hoop fan

Still the #1 legendary roots crew fan

I still trip and fall and hang sideways off the wall

But the trip is nice and I'm humble for it all

All in all I'm still me and wonder things too like

That day etched by a memory

Because I reminisce over you fa real.

By Chyren Hayes ©3/15/05

The Inspirations behind Brown Skin

The inspiration behind Brown skin can be called an ironic mislabeling. It started with a song I heard by Blackstar called "brownskin lady". I always had an attraction for dark brown pretty sista's ever since I could remember. So just the word brownskin in itself was just used to describe that type of a sista. I was kicking it with this light skinned lady friend named Bridgette and while talking to her I said whats up Brown skin. It was a reflex and actually that phrase slipped out because I took her to be light skin. But she was like naw brotha I'm brown skin. She got a kick out of me calling her brown skin so I just kept it up.(She thought it was sweet). I carried the nickname on as I met other sistas because hey a brotha loves a brown skin lady. In comes Tootie. I was really feeling this woman. And it seems that a lot of times when I write exactly what I'm feeling the words come out more fluently. I had been stuck trying to write a poem for a long time and just got frustrated with coming up with nothing. Then I started to think about her and the rest is in black and white.

Brown Skin

I met this brown skin affection

Once I made the decision to do for self

She caught me by a smile

And I was hers more or less

I introduced the idea of getting together, soon at best

I'm interested in getting to know you, me I'm just fresh

I'm short brown and them some

Spirit easy like The Good Son

I seek knowledge and understanding, wisdom, love and have fun

I saw your spirit open fly free, in front of me

And with a body like that, I said yeah she could be with me

My wisdom spoke to my heart and my heart spoke to my mind

I thought what would be pleasing to the ear of her Empress divine

So I spoke exactly and firm, Honest and True

Now we collaborate on topics on topics of understanding

Each day feels brand new

She mothers two seeds with direction

and for herself she draws strength

Oh how I admire power and beauty, it inspires the man in me

And Love is Love in a circle now Earth, Moon and Sun.

We orchestrate harmony in unison

on different levels of communication

Now I write like I'm filled with new life, lines off the top

The more emotion I put into the harder I rock

I wonder if I found my better half

Cause two halves make whole

The old man did say, "Let your spirit go and go with the flow."

And if you're "fee ing good energy just walk through the door'

Hmm so this is what it feels like …honest and pure.

By Chyren Hayes © 8/26/00

The Inspiration behind In this New Life of Mine

The inspiration behind "In This New Life of Mine" was from a wedding request that came from a woman I worked with. I was really getting a lot of attention and love from my coworkers and requests were coming in left and right. This poem wasn't actually hard to come up with for some reason. God bless that. I'm not sure if I was in the groove or if I felt close to the subject but it came fairly easy. I believe it took me about 2 days to complete. On a side note, some years later I also gave a copy of this poem as a wedding gift to my man Kurt Renfroe and his wife. God works in mysterious ways.

In This New Life of Mine

In this new life of mine

I share with you gifts from divine

My heart speaks pleasure when I share your time

I give unto thee forever till thine

Until thy kingdom come from now thus - we will be one

I honor you as a gift given from His Holy Son

A reflection of Love, As I have loved Him with no exception

An Image of my faith has so appeared in the flesh

More heavenly than I imagined I have now seen His Bless

In this new life of mine

I can only promise you Forever

That by your side I will be, Through the storms of the weather

And when impure emotions knocks at the entrance of our Home

I will stand to cast them away

and pronounce that here Love has a strong hold

I promise to accept you for all that you are

From in-with to with-out you are my heart

In this new life of mine

I have found love within myself

So much so taking life in precious breathes

So as I find myself in jubilee, Sincerely I ask you with a kiss

In this New Life of Mine

Would you be the person I share the rest of my life with?

By Chyren Hayes©5/4/99

The Inspiration behind When I was in Love

The inspiration behind When I was in love is simply in the title of the poem. I wrote this for myself. I think somewhere along the lines I figured out that I don't have a problem finding words or the emotions to express the girl-boy relationship thing. I found that although I can write from a fictitious place or dramatize some ideas the thoughts are more readily available when I write on relationships. This poem is about how I met my first love with those beginning experiences and courting.

When I was in Love

She struck me like an instance

Stuck standing observing her from a distance

It was inviting yet hesitant but familiar

It was a-alikeness I had seen before

Often or more peace and love flourished

She took me from consciousness many nights with allure'

Away to her and all that a young man wishes his life to be

Full with the truest kind of….act of…Take this as a memento of…

Sharing and giving, calvary and chivalry

An epiphany pondered upon me

As in knowledge born or from uncommon to the most likely

Propensity, I was inclined towards the direction of she

Introduction made acquaintance and acquaintance made friends

We became so nice like hip-hop now she the love of my life

We were deep into conversations under orange skies, starry nights

Full moons, how big is the sea

and who we wanted to grow to be like

I was in love with her brown skin eyes, brown skin smile

She looked at the world like a brown skin innocent child

We were into saying peace & hair grease,

exploring ourselves and being free

She was 90% of my time and 100% on my mind

I remember walking to her house after work late nights many times

It was a blessing finding an a-alikeness of my reflection

I started exploring art and writing poetry

Music was her passion and she'd play different songs for me

Back when I was in love with her Everyday was a new song

Not what she played but my heart sung its own

We used to sip bottles of wine, lose focus and lose time

We were lost in love, wrapped into each other,

2 bodies with 1 mind

By Chyren Hayes © 10-21-02

The Inspiration behind Right Here

The inspiration behind Right Here was a request from a homeboy I went to college with, Benny Austin. I graduated Newberry College in '93 (Alpha phi Alpha is the frat) and met some of my closet homeboys there. I was visiting a few of those homeboys in Columbia, SC one weekend while living here in Atlanta. Once I let it be known I was doing spoken word and showcased a piece for them Benny asked me to write one for him. The point of it was he was trying to gain this girl's attention to look at him being more than just friends. It seemed simple to come up with the title called Right here. I can't say if Benny was super pleased or if it ever made a difference between him and the girl. All I can actually say is you can read it Right Here.

Right Here

I've been wanting to tell you some things I think you oughta know

Going through my mind it has been for sometime

Together we've been without a situation #9

Building ties closer like shoelaces when they unwind

It's been igging me to show you but I wonder if you see

That sometimes right in front of you

is where the answer tends to be

I'm sure hard luck and bad times put a strain on the eyes

But what I'm trying to say is I'm right here like sunshine

Like your old high school teacher you hadn't seen in years

Or that thirty-five cents underneath the driver seat

 – I'm still Right Here

I'm Right Here like soul train on Saturdays even at the same time

Or your girlfriend you hadn't talk to

since you had trouble on the mind

I'm right here like the keys on the dresser

when you're looking right pass it

Or that book you never read even

although everyday you look right at it

Like that pair of shoes you keep just in case you might need

Or those old pair of jeans that's wore out in the knees

I'm right here like your home town

because you know ain't nothing change

Or your old school crew that still right there doing the same thing

Like those student loans you've been paying

for what seems like forever

Or that pain in your leg you thought was gone

but is right there with the weather

I know our relations is a casual situation

But I'm just asking to look at me closer

and recognize whom your facing

Sometimes the greatest thing could be just what you don't see

But until that change I'll be Right Here - Being me

BY Chyren Hayes © 6/27/00

The Inspiration behind I love Her

I think this is a beautiful poem. After years of having it I have yet to perform this piece. I have it framed in my house for all who enters to see. It was inspired by the classic hip hop song "I Used to love H.E.R" by Common - another beautiful song. This poem came to me at a time when I was feeling down on myself about the failed relationships I had been having. I was feeling alone and sorta lonely. I thought back to what has been consistent in my life and released it in my poetry.

I Love Her

Since as long as I can remember

you've always been a part of my life

Not really knowing who you were

sometimes when I see you I pass you by

Stopping rarely to talk but when we did it always came easy

It took a long time for me to figure out

the time we shared always pleased me

I think you were sent to me sometime back in elementary

And when you came up out the mouth

 I thought it was all because of me then I left you for a while

because life is a trip that took me on the road

I'm experimenting with all kinds of things

while others I had no control

Seeing Life in the expanded, I'm getting older

and one day you tapped me on the shoulder

Good timing now because feelings put on paper

always seem to stand out bolder

Not really sure why you came back or if you ever left

They say True Love always comes back home

and for that God Bless

You helped me through so many hard times

I owe you so much more than I can give

When I was trying to find myself

We walked through so many doors and you escorted me in.

You never judged me or shun me

when I was down you opened up your arms

And when I wanted to spread love you gave me two extra arms

I see that together we go hand in hand like a pen and a pad

If it wasn't for you I wouldn't be who I am today

Strong and in Demand

I'm loving you now and I'll cherish you for all that you are

I didn't know it then but we were committed to each other

right from the start

May God Bless this union for always and keep it fresh and exciting

The Day I realize that My Love is my writing.

By Chyren Hayes © 5/13/99

The Inspiration behind From Far Away

The inspiration behind From Far Away is a surprised gift to an old girlfriend. We were at a point where we were close and I wanted to do something I always wanted which is send a poem and some flowers to a woman at her job. Well I decided that instead of thinking about doing it to just do it. But would you believe after waiting about two weeks for a response I called her to ask if she got the gift I sent and she never got the poem. She told me her job prohibits them from receiving gifts since she worked for a collection agency. I was disappointed because that would have been my ace in the hole to kind of turn the tides my way. Be that as it may things never really worked out anyway except I have this bomb ass poem to add to the catalog.

From Far Away

From Far Away

I thought I might as I remembered as I Did

Change the atmosphere of the room

with a message from you know who

From Far Away

I thought I might as I remembered as I could

Remind you of His loving arms in these times,

Just as a man should

From Far Away

I thought I might as I remembered as I can

Put it in black and white so Loud you feel when you stand

I wondered if I still could as I wrote this today

Put a smile on your face by someone who is

From Far Away.

By Chyren Hayes © 1/5/01

The Inspiration behind I finally have found

The inspiration behind I finally have found is from a request from a lady co-worker that was getting married. I had just started sharing my poems around the office by writing on birthday and sympathy greeting cards. They were surprise that I was the writer and even more surprised that the poems were pretty decent so fellow coworkers started to make request for poems. I'm sure most poets or any artist comes to deal with this type of thing every now and then. I accepted the invitation mainly because of flattery but they have no idea how much I sweat and beat myself up to squeeze out something closely resembling a poem. For this poem I put myself in the frame of mind as what I would say to my lady when I get married or at least something comparable to it. She liked the poem so much that she had it read at the wedding as a part of the ceremony. I was even more flattered and honored.

I Finally Have Found

I have been a wondering soul in search of a dream

That transcends heaven every way I had imagined it to be

Everyday I prayed to God, "Please send an angel down"

Today before you and him I confess Love, I finally have found

Our fate has met because Destiny is a wonderful thing

No man shall tear apart anything Together the Lord forth brings

God Bless a family, for you a boy and me a little girl

The Love of my life now my family is my world

I commit myself to you under the eyes of the Almighty

Tears come from my eyes

when I think of the love between you and me

Everything that I was searching for

I was blessed twice over and abound

My soul no longer wonders because Love, I finally have found

By Chyren Hayes © 12/17/96

The Inspiration behind Young Sista

The inspiration behind Young sista is a friend of mine named Shanna. We used to hang out and have the best of times back in the day. She's a little younger than me but hella sexy. As I saw her getting older she would talk to me about issues with guys, boyfriends, and her job. I could tell that she was just seeing how the world can be so cold and everyman can be for himself. So for her birthday I decided to write another scripture on her behalf hoping to inspire and to keep her on a straight path- from a young girl into a grown woman.

Young Sista

This one is dedicated to you on your birthday Young Sista,

God Bless your Life and that he always will stay with you.

Remember Life is a Gift and Blessings come in disguise,

Pray before you sleep and say another when you rise.

Think before you speak and like Jesse, "keep hope alive".

I ain' playing you'll see only the faithful and the strong survive.

Be true to self and always stand on something,

A principal or idea else you're a 'Herb' just frontin'.

Good looks and a smile will only get you in the door

Legs are cool

but hips and breast are worth just a little bit more. (Smile)

And straight off the top you mustn't forget you're "Africa's Pride"

Queens still walk the Ghetto.

Remember Angela Davis, Nina Simon and Lauryn Hill right.?

Respect yourself and the rest of those bustas will follow suite

And those that aren't ready let'em see how you betty-boop.

And as Far as You and I, we're forever related.

Committed in a form that one of us is not appreciating.

Ignoring a true fact that I hope I don't one day regret.

My feelings for you are there

but our age right now is a prime suspect.

May God forgive me if I'm wrong.

I never wanted to hurt anyone (I know what that's like).

I only wanted to have Love and write about it in a poem.

Happy Birthday Young Sista,

God willing there's rewards in faithful living,

A lesson for you and me "Do you hear him talking?"

I think we ought to Listen!

By Chyren Hayes ©11/15/99

The Inspiration behind My Notebook and Me

The inspiration behind My Notebook and Me is having an honest, true discussion and reflective look with myself. I periodically write in a diary to keep practicing expressing my emotions with words. One night I was letting it all out and I was feeling extremely good and relieved. I also had been inflicted with writers block. When I have things heavy on the mind I could never set out to write a poem or even finish one for that matter. It just never works out. Writing in my journal gives me an avenue to release and just maybe I can write a small poem. At the end of this entry I just felt the motion of the ocean in me and instead of talking to myself in poetic verse (as I always do) I just started writing what I was saying and kept writing. I found myself three quarters through when I realized how much and how clear and concise it was. I think it's one of the truest depictions of how I see myself.

My Notebook & Me

It's been a while since we talked amongst ourselves;

My Notebook & Me.

We used to be intimate about it the daily expressing it on the Free.

No lines to formulate just feelings to expressly make

But I miss you dearly, it's still only you and me really

Although I fantasize about a life living well

At times it seems I'm still fantasizing just as well

I'm older than I used to be so it implies that I've grown

But actually I still feel like a kid lost out in the world.

I'm not sure if I really recovered from the ending of my last

Since she's been gone I hadn't had anyone more than a minute

Or else I just keep letting them pass

Years go by and I wonder if there's something wrong with me

Figure there's got to be a reason;

a new house, a new job and still a lonely me.

So I greet'em like I meet'em and I leav'em like I don't need'em

But that's only tit for tat; I'm moving

But getting nowhere without any reason.

So now it's intricately thought out

And now I've learned to just be free

But I must've learned what I wanna learn

because it seems it's still only me

I stop sexing like I'm religious but God knows I still get the feeling

I meet 3rd class females who actually are mentally appealing

It's like I'm caught up on looks but then I'm passing up azz

So I can't win for loosing

but I still pray at night hoping today is the last

Somehow hopeful dreams still make up me.

'Everyday I dream' will soon be real.

But all in all I can't be mad.

Fun times & sad, I guess it all makes me a man.

Honestly I gotta say I'm probably glad it's still my notebook & me

Because If someone else came along

I wonder wouldn't we slowly drift away like the breeze?

My Notebook & Me

By Chyren Hayes ☺ 9/19/00

Suga Listen

On This Valentine

LOST

Matters of My heart

In Wonder Why

LOVE

Don't Ask Me

The Inspiration behind Suga Listen

The inspiration behind Sugar Listen is a simple sense of urgency. I was crazy interested in this girl named Liberia. I was sure we had some kind of connection from my attempts to get closer. But being overzealous and persistent I jumped way to conclusions or someone really did throw salt in my game. In hindsight it was the former. She started giving me the cold shoulder. So I wrote this poem to state my case in efforts to get back to good vibes. But to no glorious ends because in the end it seems I was just imagining everything from the start. All in all I learned about perception, small talk, persistence and actual real conversation. Also I learned how I people just switch up. Actually I like this poem because it shows one example out of the countless thousands how feelings stimulate beautiful creativity. And more so than that I'm especially glad I was able to add another poem to my catalogue. Thanks Liberia.

Suga Listen

A misunderstanding, I never intended for it to be,

I only wanted us together enjoying our company.

Somehow sidetracked, either deliberate or tripped,

The first smile that you gave I saw a twinkle in it.

It was a feeling, that took me from depths and brought me up,

I saw the future in your eyes and wishing for one Love.

A tragic flaw, If only you'll listen and understand,

These turning points of events was never part of my plan.

Sugar listen, Playa haters and snakes are in disguise,

Wanting another mans heaven and wishing for his demise.

I've made mistakes, but only in efforts to do what's right,

Can you blame me if I tried and it never came out right?

Now its twisted, I can't even be heard because of noise,

But still I'm coming through like a fleet of convoys.

And steady mobbin', Making you feel me with these words,

If anything is left I'ma have the last words.

A man standing, saying his peace with a piece,

Can't you see that I'm sincere and want this drama to cease?

Suga Listen, just give it a minute to think it through,

I'd rather be writing bomb poems about being with you.

By Chyren Hayes © 8/10/07

The Inspiration behind Matter of My Heart

The inspiration behind this poem is a combination of three things. At the time I was still looking over my shoulder to get back with an old girlfriend. You know how we try to lie to ourselves. I'm not ashamed to say it because we all do it. But that was then and now I've moved past that. I decided to actually put the words on paper because I still was stuck on in a space and couldn't write about anything else. And all writers know that if your mind is someplace then you're pretty much halted there until you deal with that. And since all the well known writers, poets, musician and spoken word artist I admire says write everything down I tried it. The title was inspired from reading lots of love poems in books and on the web. I figured it would work.

Matters of My Heart

On The Matters of My heart,

I don't feel much like love anymore

I don't feel like love loves me anymore

I feel lost and burnt out forever more

I feel sad and bruised, hurt and obscure

I feel like crying a whole lot more

I feel less and less sure and more insecure

I'm trying to put it together smarter than I ever did before

I'm the biggest faker if there ever was one before

I'm broke down and scared as if I was in war

If I said I didn't love her I wouldn't be pure

I'm missing her more and more,

Time takes me Either, With, And, Along, or Or

If there ever was a thing to fall victim, I fell for it, sure.

I'm confused, turned around, bamboozled and led astray

Temptations with an indecisive nature, I'm fighting to stay away

With all my hope and all my heart,

I pray one day for a brand new start

Love, forgive my faith in this poem but

The Matters of my Heart are worn.

By Chyren Hayes ©1999

The Inspiration behind Don't Ask

The inspiration for Don't Ask me was a skit I saw on the classic T.V show In Living Color by Kim Wayans. She plays this lady who talks about people business but starts off by saying "now you ain't heard it from me but". I was also imagining myself talking to a kid and knowing that one day this kid is gonna have to deal with love and all the ups and downs that come with it.

Don't Ask Me

If you never been in love then Don't ask me

Because I'll tell you seldom is the future of true L.O.V.E

The masses know and the young are yet to learn

That in a lifetime, by Love you will be burned

Don't Ask me because I'll tell you what you don't wanna hear

Good things comes to those who wait

but at the same time Life is not fair

The future is promised with riches,

everything you ever wanted avoiding the ditches.

Some say the cards you get dealt others say the way you play them

Determines if you get hemmed in stitches.

Optimistic with faith and you better not lose your religion

Because believing in something then abandoning it is a cardinal sin

So it's not like I'm saying your

Dammed if you do and dammed if you're don't.

But DAMM, if you do and DAMMED if you don't.

Don't ask me because I'll tell you

love is the greatest thing a man could have

But at the same time,

 Is it better to have Loved then to not have had?

Being in love is a righteous emotion

Then again when it's gone it leaves behind jealously, envy,

drama, and just plain commotion.

Don't ask me because I'll tell you in, out, over and done

Is the way to handle a situation like that.

You hadn't heard it from me but most times your far from over and

years from done when love jumps on your back.

I know I couldn't tell you completely what Love is,

but that's just a matter of respect.

Don't ask me but when you fall in love,

You'll know because it's something you feel deep inside yourself.

By Chyren Hayes ©5/17/00

The Inspiration behind On This Valentine

The inspiration behind On This Valentine is interesting. I knew Valentine's Day was fast approaching and I had been thinking with this talent I have I really could make a girl happy. But since I didn't have a girl I wasn't feeling my best. I was also trying to keep the writing moving by writing every chance I get. For some reason I was always on that type of mentality. I decided that since I didn't have a girl to call my own I would write what it was like not having one on Valentine' Day. I didn't put too much effort in this poem except when it came time to share it some years later. I was sorta embarrassed to let anyone know I felt that way. Now I just see it as the order of things and everyone has those feelings. I also have another one for the catalog and God bless that.

On This Valentine

Red roses, balloons, cards and chocolate

Pink hearts and ribbons I never seem to get.

But a show with a song and a good beat to dance

Are mostly the options that are left to my chance.

So I made the part seem better than its whole

Making out good sitting here completely all alone.

See I'm flying free - man I'm just fine

Even though my heart hurts on this Valentine.

Hugs and kisses, love and best wishes

No one to call my own so nobody's listening.

But I ain't tripping, I think cupid got the problem

I got a lonely heart and he ain't trying to solve it.

So my sweetest poems, I'll write tomorrow

Today it's just a story of a valentine sorrow.

By Chyren Hayes ©2/8/98

The Inspiration behind In Wonder Why

The inspiration behind In Wonder Why is at its basic- a self evaluation. I wrote this because I was questioning why an old girlfriend was really friendly with me. I was always thinking negative and suspect about our friendship and thought she was spending time with me under false pretenses. No one wants to play the fool and I didn't want to either. Another source of inspiration for this poem was my re-reading a lot of the English literature poetry I read in college. I was reading a lot of Emily Dickinson, Ralph Emerson, etc. I was challenging myself to be like them. I had this crazy idea that if I called myself a poet I should be able to write in the style they did. So if you check the format of the poem it's my attempt to pattern the poem in that vein.

In Wonder Why

I find myself in wonder why

We stand together side by side.

It does me best to think that she

Found her heart truly lies with me.

But Dark and doubt has crept in slow

Whispering what they think I ought to know.

Her prior past not lived as plan

Cause found her lover in other's hand.

Faked and tricked her heart is hit.

But leave is not an option since

Mind & Soul with Body enwrapped

Around his finger like this and like that.

But roots grow thin when nurture is gone

So courage to break a spell grows strong.

As Time has past heart weary at last

Sad to leave but must if she'll last.

So Now I find myself in wonder why

She stands by me at my side.

It does me best to think that she

Found her heart truly lies with me.

By Chyren Hayes ©2/1/00

Acknowledgments

I want to thank my immediate family; my dear mother Barbara Forrest, my beautiful sister L'corius Hayes, my brother Marion Hayes, and my enterprising cousin (just like a brother) Lamont Mcgill. We all started from the same place, 7 ½ Kracke st., Charleston, SC. We were just little kids playing outside until the lights came on. As a kid I always would stare across the Ashley River and look up into the night time sky and made grand wishes. God Bless our family and another wish has come through.

She'ree and Wanda from GTECH for that 1st big push of encouragement and acceptance to share my writings. It was all in my notebook before you two.

A special thanks to Cheneque(CJ), Bridgett and Serena, who are my biggest supporters and seeing something in my work that warranted special attention. I deeply appreciate you.

To my Uncle Earnest King, get well soon. You gave my art a sense of validity. I'll always cherish that Khalil Gibran book you gave me after reading my work.

To those who bear my request to review my latest poem and to tell me what you think. Thanks for your patience and understanding that it's just my passion.

I can't forget any of the open mic's I've touched through the years
I've met so many poets, musicians, producers, mc's, rappers, singers, amateurs, semi-pro, night time entertainers and those that have gone on to stages around the globe and television and continue to promote the art. We really only do it for the Love for the Art.

Story of Cover Art

A big thank you to Gilbert Young for your cover design for this book. Everyone should know this story. Mr. Young was at the bar with his wife while I sat on the other side. Each of us were oblivious to who the other was. The bartender slide a sketch to me you drew on a napkin. He says do you know who that is? That's Gilbert Young. He drew "He aint Heavy". You should keep it. I did. I framed it. Years later I reached out to you to refresh your memory abou that faithful day and to get your permission. It is an honor and a blessing. Thank you.

Chyren Hayes is a poet and spoken word artist born and raised in
 Charleston, South Carolina. He is a graduate of Newberry College with a bachelor's degree in Mathematics and Computer Science. Professionally he is trained as an application support technician. He started writing poetry as a hobby around sixteen yrs old motivated by teenage love and urban music. In a college English Literature class his respect and appreciation for the art grew where he was formally introduced to a broader range and the technical aspects of poetry. He began sharing his style of writings on the extraordinary open-mic scenes in Atlanta, GA where he currently resides. He has performed at the now defunct Yin Yang Cafe', Apache Café', Nuyorican Poets Café. He has been published in Rolling out Weekly newspaper. He has appeared as a guest on radio station 88.5 WRFG poetry show and V-103 quiet storm with Joyce Little. He has performed at different religious functions and church's', Delta Sigma Sorority Annual fundraiser and at The Annual Big Brother Big Sister picnic. In his spare time he is an avid NBA fan that still likes to play pick-up games. He loves to learn anything about art, history and culture.